A GIFT FOR

---

FROM

---

# Max Lucado

# Safe *in the* Shepherd's Arms

Hope & Encouragement *from Psalm 23*

Thomas Nelson
*Since 1798*

NASHVILLE   DALLAS   MEXICO CITY   RIO DE JANEIRO

*Safe in the Shepherd's Arms*
Copyright © 2002, 2009 by Max Lucado

Published in Nashville, Tennessee, by Thomas Nelson®. Thomas Nelson® is a registered trademark of Thomas Nelson, Inc.

All rights reserved. No portion of this publication may be reproduced, stored in a retrieval system, or transmitted by any means—electronic, mechanical, photocopying, recording, or any other—except for brief quotations in printed reviews, without the prior written permission of the publisher.

Thomas Nelson, Inc. titles may be purchased in bulk for educational, business, fund-raising, or sales promotional use. For information, please e-mail SpecialMarkets@ThomasNelson.com.

Unless otherwise noted, all Scripture references are from New Century Version® (NCV). © 2005 by Thomas Nelson, Inc. Used by permission. All rights reserved.

Other Scripture references are taken from HOLY BIBLE, NEW INTERNATIONAL VERSION® (NIV). Copyright © 1973, 1978, 1984 by International Bible Society. Used by permission of Zondervan Publishing House. All rights reserved.

NEW KING JAMES VERSION (NKJV). © 1979, 1980, 1982, 1992, Thomas Nelson, Inc.

THE NEW ENGLISH BIBLE (NEB). © 1961, 1970, by The Delegates of the Oxford University Press and the Syndics of the Cambridge University Press. Reprinted by permission.

Today's English Version (TEV). © 1966, 1971, 1976, 1992 by the American Bible Society.

*Holy Bible*, New Living Translation (NLT). © 1996. Used by permission of Tyndale House Publishers, Inc., Wheaton, Ill. All rights reserved.

*The Message* by Eugene H. Peterson (MSG). © 1993, 1994, 1995, 1996, 2000. Used by permission of NavPress Publishing Group.

*The Living Bible* (TLB). © 1971. Used by permission of Tyndale House Publishers, Wheaton, IL. All rights reserved.

Editorial Supervision: Karen Hill, Executive Editor for Max Lucado

Designed by Koechel Peterson & Associates, Minneapolis, MN

ISBN-13: 978-1-4041-8771-9

Printed and bound in China

www.thomasnelson.com

12 13 14 15 [RRD] 10 9 8 7

FOR PAT HILE

*Celebrating twenty years of faithful service to the same flock*

{ TABLE OF CONTENTS

INTRODUCTION

The Lord Is My Shepherd ............................................................. 10

I Shall Not Want ........................................................................ 18

He Makes Me to Lie Down in Green Pastures ........................... 24

He Leads Me Beside Still Waters ................................................ 30

He Restores My Soul ................................................................... 34

He Leads Me in Paths of Righteousness ..................................... 40

For His Name's Sake .................................................................... 44

Yea, Though I Walk through the Valley
of the Shadow of Death ...................................................... 48

I Will Fear No Evil ..................................................................... 54

Thou Art with Me ....................................................................... 60

Your Rod and Your Staff, They Comfort Me ............................ 64

You Prepare a Table Before Me
in the Presence a My Enemies ............................................. 70

You Anoint My Head with Oil .................................................... 74

My Cup Runs Over ...................................................................... 84

Surely Goodness and Mercy Shall Follow Me
All the Days of My Life ........................................................ 90

I Will Dwell in the House of the Lord Forever ..................... 98

Closing Thoughts ....................................................................... 104

30-Day Devotional ....................................................................... 109

INTRODUCTION }

"Come to me," God invites, "all of you who are weary and carry heavy burdens, and I will give you rest" (Matthew 11:28 NLT).

If we let him, God will lighten our loads… but how do we let him? May I invite an old friend to show us? The Twenty-third Psalm.

*The LORD is my shepherd;*
  *I shall not want.*
*He makes me to lie down in green pastures;*
  *He leads me beside the still waters.*
*He restores my soul;*
  *He leads me in the paths of righteousness*
  *For His name's sake.*
*Yea, though I walk through the valley of the*
  *shadow of death,*
  *I will fear no evil;*
  *For You are with me;*
  *Your rod and Your staff, they comfort me.*
*You prepare a table before me*
  *in the presence of my enemies;*
  *You anoint my head with oil;*
  *My cup runs over.*
*Surely goodness and mercy shall follow me*
  *All the days of my life;*
  *And I will dwell in the house of the Lord Forever.* (NKJV)

Do more beloved words exist? Framed and hung in hospital rooms, scratched on prison walls, quoted by the young, and whispered by the dying. In these lines, sailors have found a harbor, the frightened have found a father, and strugglers have found a friend.

And because the passage is so deeply loved, it is widely known. Can you find ears on which these words have never fallen? Set to music in a hundred songs, translated into a thousand tongues, domiciled in a million hearts.

One of those hearts might be yours.

Max Lucado

# The Lord Is My Shepherd

The psalmist rejoiced to say, "The Lord is my shepherd," and in so doing he proudly implied, "I am his sheep."

Why did David write the Twenty-third Psalm? To build our trust in God… to remind us of who he is. Yahweh— an unchanging God, and uncaused God, and an ungoverned God.

When Lloyd Douglas, author of *The Robe* and other novels, attended college, he lived in a boardinghouse. A retired, wheelchair-bound music professor resided on the first floor. Each morning Douglas would stick his head in the door of the teacher's apartment and ask the same question, "Well, what's the good news?" The old man would pick up his tuning fork, tap it on the side of the wheelchair, and say, "That's middle C! It was middle C yesterday; it will be middle C tomorrow; it will be middle C a thousand years from now. The tenor upstairs sings flat. The piano across the hall is out of tune, but, my friend, that is middle C."[1]

You and I need a middle C. Haven't you had enough change in your life? Relationships change. Health changes. The weather changes. But the Yahweh who ruled the earth last night is the same Yahweh who rules it today. Same convictions. Same plan. Same mood. Same love. He never changes. You can no more alter God than a pebble can alter the rhythm of the Pacific. Yahweh is our middle C. A still point in a turning world. Don't we need a still point? Don't we need an unchanging shepherd?

We equally need an uncaused shepherd. No one breathed life into Yahweh. No one sired him. No one gave birth to him. No one caused him. No act brought him forth.

Though he creates, God was never created. Though he makes, he was never made. Though he causes, he was never caused. Hence the psalmist's proclamation: "Before the mountains were born or you brought forth the earth and the world, from everlasting to everlasting you are God" (Psalm 90:2 NIV).

God—our Shepherd—doesn't check the weather; he makes it. He doesn't defy gravity; he created it. He isn't affected by health; he has no body. Jesus said, "God is spirit" (John 4:24). Since he has no body, he has no limitations—equally active in Cambodia as he is in Connecticut. "Where can I go to get away from your Spirit?" asked David. "Where can I run from you? If I go up to the heavens, you are there. If I lie down in the grave, you are there" (Psalm 139:7–8).

Since no act brought him forth, no act can take him out. Does he fear an earthquake? Does he tremble at a tornado? Hardly. Yahweh sleeps through storms and calms the winds with a word. Cancer does not trouble him and cemeteries do not disturb him. He was here before they came. He'll be here long after they are gone….

*God doesn't check the weather; he makes it. He doesn't defy gravity; he created it.*

Counselors can comfort you in the storm, but you need a God who can still the storm. Friends can hold your hand at your deathbed, but you need a Yahweh who has defeated the grave. Philosophers can debate the meaning of life, but you need a Lord who can declare the meaning of life.

You need a Yahweh.

You don't need what Dorothy found. Remember her discovery in *The Wonderful Wizard of Oz*? She and her trio followed the yellow brick road only to discover that the wizard was a wimp! Nothing but smoke and mirrors and tin-drum thunder. Is that the kind of god you need?

You don't need to carry the burden of a lesser god…a god on a shelf, a god in a box, or a god in a bottle. No, you need a God who can place 100 billion stars in our galaxy and 100 billion galaxies in the universe. You need a God who can shape two fists of flesh into 75 to 100 billion nerve cells, each with as many as 10,000 connections to other nerve cells, place it in a skull, and call it a brain.

And you need a God who, while so mind-numbingly might, can come in the soft of night and touch you with the tenderness of April snow.

You need Yahweh.

And, according to David, you have one. He is your Shepherd.

TRAVELING LIGHT

*You are a great God.*
*Your character is holy.*
*Your truth is absolute.*
*Your strength is unending.*
*Your discipline is fair....*
*Your provisions are abundant for our needs.*
*Your light is adequate for our path.*
*Your grace is sufficient for our sins....*
*You are never early, never late....*
*You sent your Son in the fullness of time and*
*will return at the consummation of time.*
*Your plan is perfect.*
*Bewildering. Puzzling. Troubling.*
*But perfect.*

> From "He Reminded Us of You"
> *(A prayer for a friend)*

# I Shall Not Want

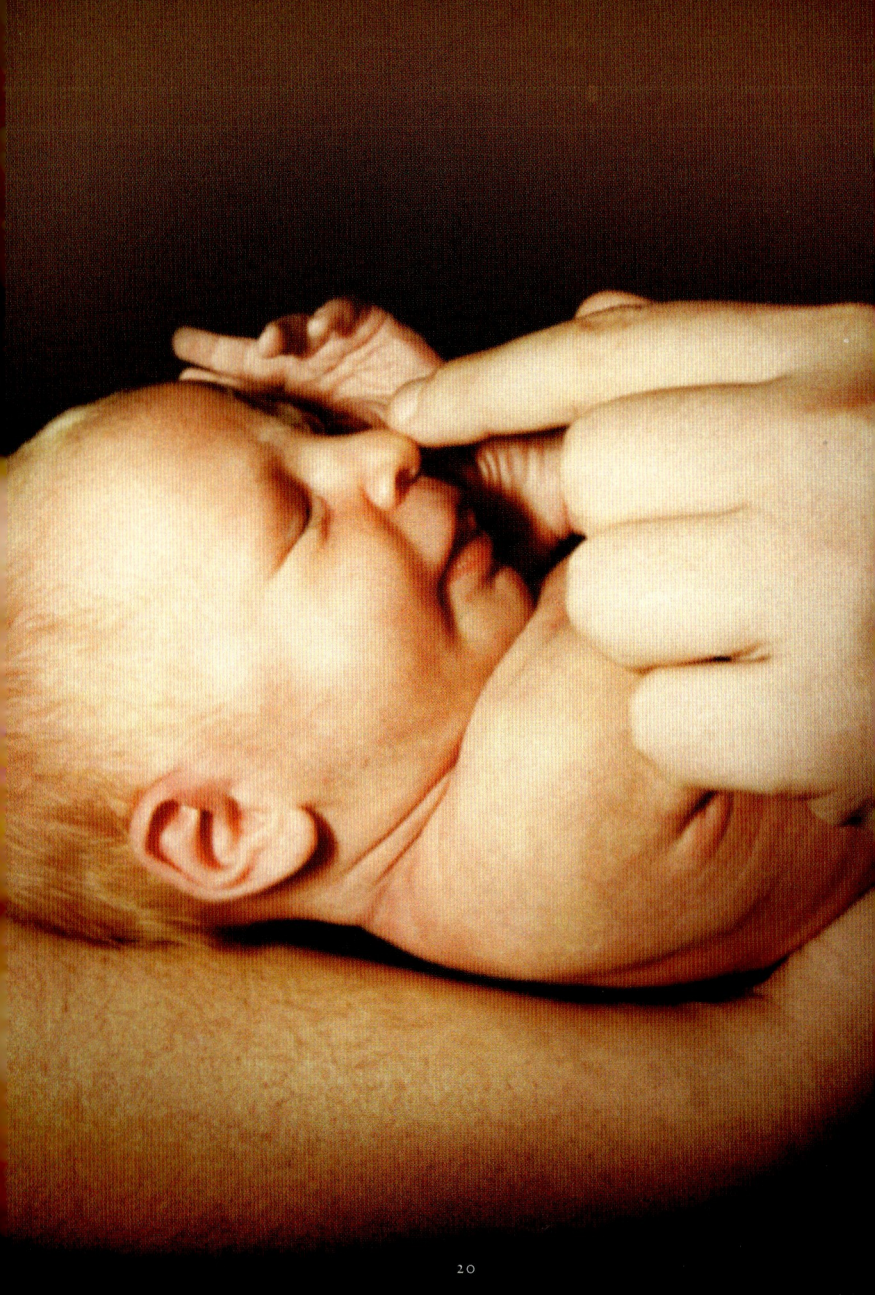

**D**AVID HAS FOUND THE PASTURE where discontent goes to die. It's as if he is saying, "What I have in God is greater than what I don't have in life."

You think you and I could learn to say the same?

Think for just a moment about the things you own. Think about the house you have, the car you drive, the money you've saved. Think about the jewelry you've inherited and the stocks you've traded and the clothes you've purchased. Envision all your stuff, and let me remind you of two biblical truths.

Your stuff isn't yours. Ask any coroner. Ask any embalmer. Ask any funeral home director. No one takes anything with him. When one of the wealthiest men in history, John D. Rockefeller, died, his accountant was asked, "How much did John D. leave?" The accountant's reply? "All of it."

"Naked a man comes from his mother's womb, and as he comes, so he departs. He takes nothing from his labor that he can carry in his hand" (Ecclesiastes 5:15 NIV).

*When God thinks of you, he doesn't think of your things.*

All that stuff—it's not yours. And you know what else about all that stuff? It's not you. Who you are has nothing to do with the clothes you wear or the car you drive. Jesus said, "Life is not defined by what you have, even when you have a lot" (Luke 12:15 MSG). Heaven does not know you as the fellow with the nice suit or the woman with the big house or the kid with the new bike. Heaven knows your heart. "The Lord does not look at the things man looks at. Man looks at the outward appearance, but the Lord looks at the heart" (I Samuel 16:7 NIV). When God thinks of you, he may see your compassion, your devotion, your tenderness or quick mind, but he doesn't think of your things....

You have a God who hears you, the power of love behind you, the Holy Spirit within you, and all of heaven ahead of you. If you have the Shepherd, you have grace for every sin, direction for every turn, a candle for every corner, and an anchor for every storm. You have everything you need.

You and I could pray like the Puritan. He sat down to a meal of bread and water. He bowed his head and declared, "All this and Jesus too?"

Can't we be equally content? Paul says that "godliness with contentment is great gain" (1 Timothy 6:6 NIV).

When we surrender to God the cumbersome sack of discontent, we don't just give up something; we gain something. God replaces it with a lightweight, tailor-made, sorrow-resistant attaché of gratitude.

What will you gain with contentment? You may gain your marriage. You may gain precious hours with your children. You may gain your self-respect. You may gain joy. You may gain the faith to say, "The Lord is my shepherd; I shall not want."

Traveling Light

# He Makes Me to Lie Down in Green Pastures

Nestle deeply in the tall shoots of love, and there you will find rest.

FOR SHEEP TO SLEEP, everything must be just right. No predators. No tension in the flock. No bugs in the air. No hunger in the belly. Everything has to be just so.

Unfortunately, sheep cannot find safe pasture, nor can they spray insecticide, deal with the frictions, or find food. They need help. They need a shepherd to "lead them" and help them "lie down in green pastures." Without a shepherd, they can't rest.

Without the Shepherd, neither can we.

In the second verse of the Twenty-third Psalm, David the poet becomes David the artist. His quill becomes a brush, his parchment a canvas, and his words paint a picture. A flock of sheep on folded legs, encircling a shepherd. Bellies nestled deep in the long shoots of grass. A still pond on one side, the watching shepherd on the other. "He makes me to lie down in green pastures; He leads me beside the still waters" (Psalm 23:2 NKJV).

Note the two pronouns preceding the two verbs. *He* makes me…*He* leads me….

Who is the active one? Who is in charge? The shepherd. The shepherd selects the trail and prepares the pasture. The sheep's job—our job—is to watch the shepherd. With our eyes on our Shepherd, we'll be able to get some sleep. "You will keep him in perfect peace, whose mind is stayed on You" (Isaiah 26:3 NKJV).

For you to be healthy, you must rest. Slow down, and God will heal you. He will bring rest to your mind, to your body, and most of all to your soul. He will lead you to green pastures.

Green pastures were not the natural terrain of Judea. The hills around Bethlehem where David kept his flock were not lush and green. Even today they are white and parched. Any green pasture in Judea is the work of some shepherd. He has cleared the rough, rocky land. Stumps have been torn out, and brush has been burned. Irrigation. Cultivation. Such are the work of a shepherd.

Hence, when David says, "He makes me to lie down in green pastures," he is saying, "My Shepherd makes me lie down in his finished work." With his own pierced hands, Jesus created a pasture for the soul. He tore out the thorny underbrush of condemnation. He pried loose the huge boulders of sin. In their place he planted seeds of grace and dug ponds of mercy.

And he invites us to rest there. Can you imagine the satisfaction in the heart of the shepherd when, with work completed, he sees his sheep rest in the tender grass?

Can you imagine the satisfaction in the heart of God when we do the same? His pasture is his gift to us. This is not a pasture that you have made. Nor is it a pasture that you deserve. It is a gift of God.

TRAVELING LIGHT

To RECOGNIZE GOD as Lord is to acknowledge that he is sovereign and supreme in the universe. To accept him as Savior is to accept his gift of salvation offered on the cross. To regard him as Father is to go a step further. Ideally, a father is the one in your life who provides and protects. That is exactly what God has done.

God has proven himself as a faithful father. Now it falls to us to be trusting children.

HE STILL MOVES STONES

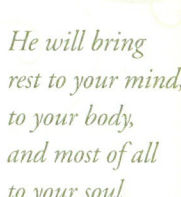

*He will bring rest to your mind, to your body, and most of all to your soul.*

# HE LEADS ME BESIDE STILL WATERS

"He leads me beside the still waters," David declares. And, in case we missed the point, he repeats the phrase in the next verse: "He leads me in the paths of righteousness."

"He leads me." God isn't behind me, yelling, "Go!" He is ahead of me, bidding, "Come!" He is in front, clearing the path, cutting the brush, showing the way. Just before the curve, he says, "Turn here." Prior to the rise, he motions, "Step up here." Standing next to the rocks, he warns, "Watch your step here."

He leads us. He tells us what we need to know when we need to know it. As a New Testament writer would affirm: "We will find grace to help us *when we need it*" (Hebrews 4:16 NLT, emphasis mine).

God leads us. God will do the right thing at the right time. And what a difference that makes….

God is leading you. Leave tomorrow's problems until tomorrow.

Arthur Hays Sulzberger was the publisher of the New York Times during the Second World War. Because of the world conflict, he found it almost impossible to sleep. He was never able to banish worries from his mind until he adopted as his motto these five words—"one step enough for me"—taken from the hymn "Lead Kindly Light."[2]

*Lead, kindly Light…*
*Keep Thou feet; I do not ask to see*
*the distant scene; one step enough for me.*

God is not going to let you see the distant scene either. So you might as well quit looking for it. He promises a lamp unto our feet, not a crystal ball into the future (Psalm 119:105). We do not need to know what will happen tomorrow. We only need to know he leads us and "we will find grace to help us when we need it" (Hebrews 4:16 NLT).

TRAVELING LIGHT

WE NEED TO HEAR that God is still in control. We need to hear that it's not over until he says so. We need to hear that life's mishaps and tragedies are not a reason to bail out. They are simply a reason to sit tight.

Corrie ten Boom used to say, "When the train goes through a tunnel and the world gets dark, do you jump out? Of course not. You sit still and trust the engineer to get you through."

Next time you're disappointed, don't panic. Don't jump out. Don't give up. Just be patient and let God remind you he's still in control. It ain't over till it's over.

HE STILL MOVES STONES

*We do not need to know what will happen tomorrow. We only need to know he leads us.*

# He Restores My Soul

JESUS RESTORES OUR HOPE BY GIVING US HIMSELF.

It's hard to see things grow old. The town in which I grew up is growing old.... Some of the buildings are boarded up. Some of the houses are torn down.... The old movie house where I took my dates has "For Sale" on the marquee....

I wish I could make it all new again. I wish I could blow the dust off the streets...but I can't.

I can't. But God can. "He restores my soul," wrote the shepherd. He doesn't reform; he restores. He doesn't camouflage the old; he restores the new. The Master Builder will pull out the original plan and restore it. He will restore the vigor. He will restore the energy. He will restore the hope. He will restore the soul.

THE APPLAUSE OF HEAVEN

*Our Shepherd majors in restoring hope to the soul.*

F OR MANY PEOPLE, life is—well, life is a jungle. Not a jungle of trees and beasts. Would that it were so simple. Would that our jungles could be cut with a machete or our adversaries trapped in a cage. But our jungles are comprised of the thicker thickets of failing health, broken hearts, and empty wallets. Our forests are framed with hospital walls and divorce courts. We don't hear the screeching of birds or the roaring of lions, but we do hear the complaints of neighbors and the demands of bosses. Our predators are our creditors, and the brush that surrounds us is the rush that exhausts us.

It's a jungle out there.

And for some, even for many, hope is in short supply….

What would it take to restore your hope?…

Our Shepherd majors in restoring hope to the soul. Whether you are a lamb lost on a craggy ledge or a city slicker alone in a deep jungle, everything changes when your rescuer appears.

Your loneliness diminishes, because you have fellowship.

You despair decreases, because you have vision.

Your confusion begins to lift, because you have direction.

Please note: You haven't left the jungle. The trees still eclipse the sky, and the storms still cut the skin. Animals lurk and rodents scurry. The jungle is still a jungle. It hasn't changed because you have hope. And you have hope because you have met someone who can lead you out.

Your shepherd knows that you were not made for this place. He knows you are not equipped for this place. So he has come to guide you out.

He has come to restore your soul….

Jesus doesn't give hope by changing the jungle; he restores our hope by giving himself. And he has promised to stay until the very end. "I am with you always, to the very end of the age" (Matthew 28:20 NIV).

Traveling Light

# He Leads Me in Paths of Righteousness

**J**ESUS CALLED HIMSELF the Good Shepherd. The Shepherd who knows his sheep by name and lays down his life for them. The Shepherd who protects, provides, and possesses his sheep. The Bible is replete with this picture of God.

> "The LORD is my shepherd" (Psalm 23:1).
>
> "We are your people, the sheep of your flock" (Psalm 79:13).
>
> "He made us, and we belong to him; we are his people, the sheep he tends" (Psalm 100:3).

The imagery is carried over to the New Testament.

> He is the shepherd who will risk his life to save the one straying sheep (see Luke 15:4).
>
> He has pity on people because they are like sheep without a shepherd (see Matthew 9:36).
>
> His disciples are his flock (see Luke 12:32).
>
> When the shepherd is attacked, the sheep are scattered (see Matthew 26:31).
>
> He is the shepherd of the souls of men (see Hebrews 13:20).

Eighty percent of Jesus' listeners made their living off of the land. Many were shepherds. They lived on the mesa with the sheep. No flock ever grazed without a shepherd, and no shepherd was ever off duty. When sheep wandered, the shepherd found them. When they fell, he carried them. When they were hurt, he healed them.

Sheep aren't smart. They tend to wander into running creeks for water, then their wool grows heavy and they drown. They need a shepherd to lead them to "calm water" (Psalm 23:2). They have no natural defense—no claws, no horns, no fangs. They are helpless. Sheep need a shepherd with a "rod and...walking stick" (Psalm 23: 4) to protect them. They have no sense of direction. They need someone to lead them "on paths that are right" (Psalm 23:3).

So do we. We, too, tend to be swept away by waters we should have avoided. We have no defense against the evil lion who prowls about seeking whom he might devour. We, too, get lost. "We all have wandered away like sheep; each of us has gone his own way" (Isaiah 53:6).

We need a shepherd. We don't need a cowboy to herd us; we need a shepherd to care for us and to guide us.

And we have one. One who knows us by name.

A Gentle Thunder

*We need a shepherd to care for us and to guide us. And we have one. One who knows us by name.*

# For His Name's Sake

GOD IS THE ONE who heals. He may use a branch of medicine and a branch of a hospital or a branch of a live oak tree, but he is the one who takes the poison out of the system. He is *Jehovah-rophe*.

He is also *Jehovah-nissi*, the Lord my banner....

These are just a few of the names of God that describe his character. Study them, for in any given day, you may need each one of them. Let me show you what I mean.

When you're confused about the future, go to your *Jehovah-raah*, your caring shepherd. When you're anxious about provision, talk to *Jehovah-jireh*, the Lord who provides. Are your challenges too great? Seek the help of *Jehovah-shalom*, the Lord is peace. Is your body sick? Are your emotions weak? *Jehovah-rophe*, the Lord who heals you, will see you now. Do you feel like a soldier stranded behind enemy lines? Take refuge in *Jehovah-nissi*, the Lord my banner.

Meditating on the names of God reminds you of the character of God. Take these names and bury them in your heart.

God is...

> the shepherd who guides,
> the Lord who provides,
> the voice who brings peace in the storm,
> the physician who heals the sick, and
> the banner that guides the soldier.

THE GREAT HOUSE OF GOD

# Yea, Though I Walk through the Valley of the Shadow of Death

Summer in ancient Palestine. A woolly bunch of bobbing heads follow the shepherd out of the gate. The morning sun has scarcely crested the horizon, and he is already leading his flock. Like every other day, he guides them through the gate and out into the fields. But unlike most days, the shepherd will not return home tonight. He will not rest on his bed, and the sheep will not sleep in their fenced-in pasture. This is the day the shepherd takes the sheep to the high country. Today he leads his flock to the mountains.

He has no other choice. Springtime grazing has left his pasture bare, so he must seek new fields. With no companion other than his sheep and no desire other than their welfare, he leads them to the deep grass of the hillsides. The shepherd and his flock will be gone for weeks, perhaps months. They will stay well into the autumn, until the grass is gone and the chill is unbearable.

Not all shepherds make this journey. The trek is long. The path is dangerous. Poisonous plants can infect the flock. Wild animals can attack the flock. There are narrow trails and dark valleys. Some shepherds choose the security of the barren pasture below.

But the good shepherd doesn't. He knows the path. He has walked this trail many times. Besides, he is prepared. Staff in hand and rod attached to his belt. With his staff he will nudge the flock; with his rod he will protect and lead the flock. He will lead them to the mountains.

David understood his annual pilgrimage. Before he led Israel, he led sheep. And could his time as a shepherd be the inspiration behind one of the greatest verses in the Bible? "Yea, though I walk through the valley of the shadow of death, I will fear no evil; for You are with me; Your rod and Your staff, they comfort me" (Psalm 23:4 NKJV).

For what the shepherd does with the flock, our Shepherd will do with us. He will lead us to the high country. When the pasture is bare down here, God will lead us up there. He will guide us through the gate, out of the flatlands, and up the path of the mountain.

Someday our Shepherd will take us to the mountain by the way of the valley. He will guide us to his house through the valley of the shadow of death.

TRAVELING LIGHT

GROWING OLDER. Aging. We laugh about it, and we groan about it. We resist it, but we can't stop it. And with the chuckles and wrinkles come some serious thoughts and questions about what happens when we die. Is death when we go to sleep? Or is death when we finally wake up?

*Is death when we go to sleep? Or is death when we finally wake up?*

As a minister, I'm often asked to speak at funerals. I no longer have to ask the family what they want me to say; I already know. Oh, I may have to ask a question or two about the deceased, and that I do, but I don't ask them what they want me to say. I know.

They want to hear what God says about death. They want to hear how God would answer their questions about the life hereafter. They don't want my opinion; nor do they want the thoughts of a philosopher or the research of a scientist. They want to know what God says. If Jesus were here, at the head of this casket, in the middle of this cemetery, what would he say?

And so under the canopy of sorrow, I give God's words. I share the eulogy Jesus gave for himself. The disciples did not know it was his farewell address. No one did, but it was. He knew he had just witnessed his final sunset. He knew death would come with the morning. So he spoke about death. Here is how he began.

*Don't let your hearts be troubled.*
*Trust in God, and trust in me. There are many*
*rooms in my Father's house; I would not tell you this if*
*it were not true. I am going there to prepare a place for you.*
*After I go and prepare a place for you,*
*I will come back and take you to be with me*
*so that you may be where I am.*
John 14:1–3

What kind of statement is that? Trust me with your death. When you face the tomb, don't be troubled—trust me! You get the impression that to God the grave is a no-brainer. He speaks as casually as the mechanic who says to a worried client, "Sure, the engine needs an overhaul, but don't worry. I can do it." For us it's an ordeal. For him it's no big deal.

We must trust God. We must trust not only that he does what is best, but that he knows what is ahead.

A GENTLE THUNDER

# I Will Fear No Evil

When I am afraid,
I will put my trust in you.

PSALM 56:3 NLT

"I WILL FEAR NO EVIL." How could David make such a claim? Because he knew where to look. "You are with me; Your rod and Your staff, they comfort me."

Rather than turn to the other sheep, David turned to the Shepherd. Rather than stare at the problems, he stared at the rod and staff. Because he knew where to look, David was able to say, "I will fear no evil."

I know a fellow who has a fear of crowds. When encircled by large groups, his breath grows short, panic surfaces, and he begins to sweat like a sumo wrestler in a sauna. He received some help, curiously, from a golfing buddy.

The two were at a movie theatre, waiting their turn to enter, when fear struck again. The crowd closed in like a forest. He wanted out and out fast. His buddy told him to take a few deep breaths. Then he helped manage the crisis by reminding him of the golf course.

"When you are hitting your ball out of the rough, and you are surrounded by trees, what do you do?"

"I look for an opening."

"You don't stare at the trees?"

"Of course not. I find an opening and focus on hitting the ball through it."

"Do the same in the crowd. When you feel the panic, don't focus on the people; focus on the opening."

Good counsel in golf. Good counsel in life. Rather than focus on the fear, focus on the solution.

That's what Jesus did.

That's what David did.

And that's what the writer of Hebrews urges us to do. "Let us run with endurance the race that is set before us, looking unto Jesus, the author and finisher of our faith" (Hebrews 12:1–2 NKJV).

Don't measure the size of the mountains; talk to the One who can move it. Instead of carrying the world on your shoulders, talk to the One who holds the universe on his. Hope is a look away.

*Rather than focus on the fear, focus on the solution.*

TRAVELING LIGHT

*Faith is trusting*
　　*what the eye can't see.*
*Eyes see the prowling lion.*
*Faith sees Daniel's angel.*
*Eyes see storms. Faith sees Noah's rainbow.*
*Eyes see giants. Faith sees Canaan.*
*Your eyes see your faults.*
*Your faith sees your Savior.*
*Your eyes see your guilt.*
*Your faith sees his blood.*
*Your eyes see your grave.*
*Your faith sees a city whose*
　　*builder and Maker is God.*
*Your eyes look in the mirror and*
　　*see a sinner, a failure, a promise-breaker.*
*But by faith you look in the mirror*
　　*and see a robed prodigal bearing the ring of*
　　*grace on your finger and the kiss of*
　　*your Father on your face.*

When God Whispers Your Name

# Thou Art with Me

"YOU ARE WITH ME."

Yes, you, Lord, are in heaven. Yes, you rule the universe. Yes, you sit upon the stars and make your home in the deep. But yes, yes, yes, you are with me.

The Lord is with me. The Creator is with me. Yahweh is with me.

Moses proclaimed it: "What great nation has a god as near to them as the LORD our God is near to us" (Deuteronomy 4:7 NLT).

Paul announced it: "He is not far from each one of us" (Acts 17:27 NIV).

And…somewhere in the pasture, wilderness, or palace, David discovered that God meant business when he said: "I will not leave you" (Genesis 28:15)….

The discovery of David is indeed the message of Scripture—the Lord is with us. And, since the Lord is near, everything is different. Everything!

*Lord, you sit upon the stars and make your home in the deep, but you are with me.*

You may be facing death, but you aren't facing death alone; the Lord is with you. You may be facing unemployment, but you aren't facing unemployment alone; the Lord is with you. You may be facing marital struggles, but you aren't facing them alone; the Lord is with you. You may be facing debt, but you aren't facing debt alone; the Lord is with you.

Underline these words: *You are not alone.*

Your family may turn against you, but God won't. Your friends may betray you, but God won't. You may feel alone in the wilderness, but you are not. He is with you.

Traveling Light

# Your Rod and Your Staff, They Comfort Me

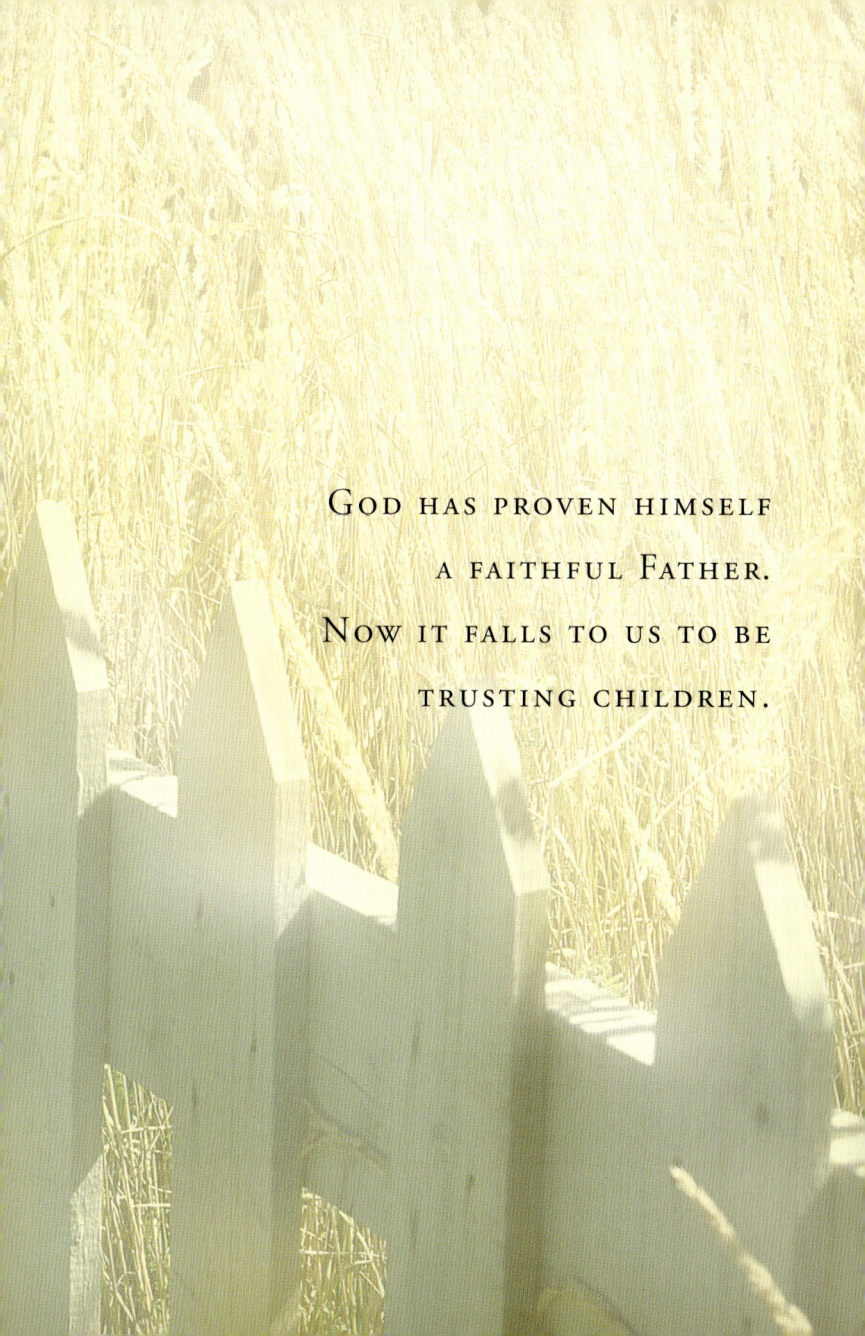

God has proven himself a faithful Father. Now it falls to us to be trusting children.

WHEN I SEE a flock of sheep I see exactly that, a flock. A rabble of wool. A herd of hooves. I don't see sheep. All alike. None different. That's what I see.

But not so with the shepherd. To him every sheep is different. Every face is special. Every face has a story. And every sheep has a name. The one with the sad eyes, that's Droopy. And the fellow with one ear up and the other down, I call him Oscar. And the small one with the black patch on his leg, he's an orphan with no brothers. I call him Joseph.

The shepherd knows his sheep. He calls them by name.

When we see a crowd, we see exactly that, a crowd. Filling a stadium or flooding a mall. When we see a crowd, we see people, not persons, but people. A herd of humans. A flock of faces. That's what we see.

But not so with the Shepherd. To him every face is different. Every face is a story. Every face is a child. Every child has a name. The one with the sad eyes, that's Sally. The old fellow with one eyebrow up and the other down, Harry's his name. And the young one with the limp? He's an orphan with no brothers. I call him Joey.

The Shepherd knows his sheep. He knows each one by name. The Shepherd knows you. He knows your name. And he will never forget it. "I have written your name on my hand" (Isaiah 49:16).

Quite a thought, isn't it? Your name on God's hand. Your name on God's lips. Maybe you've seen your name in some special places. On an award or diploma or walnut door. Or maybe you've heard your name from some important people—a coach, a celebrity, a teacher. But to think that your name is on God's hand and on God's lips…my, could it be?

WHEN GOD WHISPERS YOUR NAME

NOT ONLY is your name written on God's hand but what matters to you matters to him. You probably think that's true when it comes to the big stuff. When it comes to the major-league difficulties like death, disease, sin, and disaster—you know that God cares.

But what about the smaller things? What about grouchy bosses or flat tires or lost dogs? What about broken dishes, late flights, toothaches, or a crashed hard drive? Do these matter to God?

I mean, he's got a universe to run. He's got the planets to keep balanced and presidents and kings to watch over. He's got wars to worry with and famines to fix. Who am I to tell him about my ingrown toenail?

I'm glad you asked. Let me tell you who you are. In fact, let me proclaim who you are.

You are an heir of God and a co-heir with Christ (Romans 8:17).

You are eternal, like an angel (Luke 20:36).

You have a crown that will last forever (1 Corinthians 9:25).

You are a holy priest (1 Peter 2:5), a treasured possession (Exodus 19:5).

You were chosen before the creation of the world (Ephesians 1:4).

You are destined for "praise, fame, and honor, and you will be a holy people to the LORD your God" (Deuteronomy 26:19).

But more than any of the above—more significant than any title or position—is the simple fact that you are God's child. "The Father has loved us so much that we are called children of God. And we really are his children" (1 John 3:1).

I love that last phrase! "We really are his children." It's as if John knew some of us would shake our heads and say, "Naw, not me. Mother Teresa, maybe. Billy Graham, all right. But not me." If those are your feelings, John added that phrase for you.

"We really are his children."

As a result, if something is important to you, it's important to God.

# You Prepare a Table before Me in the Presence of My Enemies

At this point in the psalm, David's mind seems to be lingering in the high country with the sheep. Having guided the flock through the valley to the alp lands for greener grass, he remembers the shepherd's added responsibility. He must prepare the pasture.

This is new land, so the shepherd must be careful. Ideally, the grazing area will be flat, a mesa or tableland. The shepherd searches for poisonous plants and ample water. He looks for signs of wolves, coyotes, and bears.

Of special concern to the shepherd is the adder, a small brown snake that lives underground. Adders are known to pop out of their holes and nip the sheep on the nose. The bite often infects and can even kill. As defense against the snake, the shepherd pours a circle of oil at the top of each adder's hole. He also applies the oil to the noses of the animals. The oil on the snake's hole lubricates the exit, preventing the snake from climbing out. The smell of the oil on the sheep's nose drives the serpent away. The shepherd, in a very real sense, has prepared the table.[3]

What if your Shepherd did for you what the shepherd did for his flock? Suppose he dealt with your enemy, the devil, and prepared for you a safe place of nourishment? Suppose he, in the house of your failure, invited you to a meal?

What would you say if I told you he has done exactly that?

TRAVELING LIGHT

YOU SEE, he called us to himself and invited us to take a permanent place at his table. When we take our place next to the other sinners-made-saints…we share in God's glory.

May I share a partial list of what awaits you at his table?

> You are beyond condemnation (Romans 8:1).
>
> You are delivered from the law (Romans 7:6).
>
> You are near God (Ephesians 2:13).
>
> You are delivered from the power of evil (Colossians 1:13).
>
> You are justified (Romans 5:1).
>
> You have access to God at any moment (Ephesians 2:18).
>
> You will never be abandoned (Hebrews 13:5).

You possess (get this!) every spiritual blessing possible. "In Christ, God has given us every spiritual blessing in the heavenly world" (Ephesians 1:3). This is the gift offered to the lowliest sinner on earth. Who could make such an offer but God?

IN THE GRIP OF GRACE

# You Anoint My Head with Oil

When we come to God...
we come with high hopes
and a humble heart.

IN ANCIENT ISRAEL shepherds used oil for three purposes: to repel insects, to prevent conflicts, and to heal wounds.

Bugs bug people, but they can kill sheep. Flies, mosquitoes, and gnats can turn the summer into a time of torture for the livestock. Consider nose flies, for example. If they succeed in depositing their eggs into the membrane of the sheep's nose, the eggs become worm-like larvae, which drive the sheep insane. One shepherd explains: "For relief from this agonizing annoyance, sheep will deliberately beat their heads against trees, rocks, posts, or brush.... In extreme cases of intense infestation, a sheep may even kill itself in a frenzied endeavor to gain respite from the aggravation."[4]

When a swarm of nose flies appears, sheep panic. They run. They hide. They toss their heads up and down for hours. They forget to eat. They aren't able to sleep. Ewes stop milking, and lambs stop growing. The entire flock can be disrupted, even destroyed by the presence of a few flies.

For this reason, the shepherd anoints the sheep. He covers their heads with oil-like repellent. The fragrance keeps the insects at bay and the flock at peace.

At peace, that is, until mating season. Most of the year, sheep are calm, passive animals. But during mating season, everything changes. The ram puts the "ram" in *rambunctious*. They strut around the pasture and flex their necks, trying to win the attention of the new gal on the block. When a ram catches her eye, he tosses his head back and says, "I want ewe, baby." About that time her boyfriend shows up and tells her to go someplace safe. "Ewe better move, sweetie. This could get ugly." The two rams lower their heads and POW! An old-fashioned head butt breaks out.

*Be humble under God's powerful hand so he will lift you up when the right time comes.*
1 PETER 5:6

To prevent injury, the shepherd anoints the rams. He smears a slippery, greasy substance over the nose and head. This lubricant causes them to glance off rather than crash into each other.

They still tend to get hurt, however. And these wounds are the third reason the shepherd anoints the sheep.

Most of the wounds the shepherd treats are simply the result of living in a pasture. Thorns prick or rocks cut or a sheep rubs its head too hard against a tree. Sheep get hurt. As a result, the shepherd regularly, often daily, inspects the sheep searching for cuts or abrasions. He doesn't want the cut to worsen. He doesn't want today's wound to become tomorrow's infection.

Neither does God. Just like sheep, we have wounds, but ours are wounds of the heart that come from disappointment after disappointment. If we're not careful, these wounds lead to bitterness. And so just like sheep, we need to be treated. "He made us, and we belong to him; we are his people, the sheep he tends" (Psalm 100:3).

Sheep aren't the only ones who need preventive care. Sheep aren't the only ones who need a healing touch. We also get irritated with each other, butt heads, and then get wounded. Many of our disappointments in life begin as irritations. The large portion of our problems are not lion-sized attacks, but rather the day-to-day swarm of frustrations and mishaps and heartaches. You don't get invited to the dinner party. You don't make the

team. You don't get the scholarship. Your boss doesn't notice your hard work. Your husband doesn't notice your new dress. Your neighbor doesn't notice the mess in his yard. You find yourself more irritable, more gloomy, more…well, more hurt.

Like the sheep, you don't sleep well, you don't eat well. You may even hit your head against a tree a few times.

Or you may hit your head against a person. It's amazing how hardheaded we can be with each other. Some of our deepest hurts come from butting heads with people.

Like the sheep, the rest of our wounds come just from living in the pasture. The pasture of the sheep, however, is much more appealing. The sheep have to face wounds from the thorns and thistles. We have to face aging, loss, and illness. Some of us face betrayal and injustice. Live long enough in this world, and most of us will face deep, deep hurts of some kind or another.

So we, like the sheep, get wounded. And we, like the sheep, have a shepherd. Remember the words we read? "We belong to him; we are his people, the sheep he tends" (Psalm 100:3). He will do for you what the shepherd does for the sheep. He will tend to you.

If you will let him. How? How do you let him? The steps are so simple.

First, go to him. David would trust his wounds to no other person but God. He said, "You anoint my head with oil." Not, "your prophets," "your teachers," or "your counselors." Others may guide us to God. Others may help us understand God. But no one does the work of God, for only God can heal. God "heals the brokenhearted" (Psalm 147:3).

Have you taken your disappointments to God? You've shared them with your neighbor, your relatives, your friends. But have you taken them to God? James says, "Anyone who is having troubles should pray" (James 5:13).

Before you go anywhere else with your disappointments, go to God.

Maybe you don't want to trouble God with your hurts. *After all, he's got famines and pestilence and wars; he won't care about my little struggles,* you think. Why don't you let him decide that? He cared enough about a wedding to provide the wine. He cared enough about Peter's tax payment to give him a coin. He cared enough about the woman at the well to give her answers. "He cares about you" (1 Peter 5:7).

Your first step is to go to the right person. Go to God. Your second step is to assume the right posture. Bow before God.

In order to be anointed, the sheep must stand still, lower their heads, and let the shepherd do his work. Peter urges us to "be humble under God's powerful hand so he will lift you up when the right time comes" (1 Peter 5:6).

When we come to God, we make requests; we don't make demands. We come with high hopes and a humble heart. We state what we want, but we pray for what is right. And if God gives us the prison of Rome instead of the mission of Spain, we accept it because we know "God will always give what is right to his people who cry to him night and day, and he will not be slow to answer them" (Luke 18:7).

We go to him. We bow before him, and we *trust in him*.

The sheep doesn't understand why the oil repels the flies. The sheep doesn't understand how the oil heals the wounds. In fact, all the sheep knows is that something happens in the presence of the shepherd. And that's all we need to know as well. "LORD, I give myself to you; my God, I trust you" (Psalm 25:1–2).

Go. Bow. Trust.

Worth a try, don't you think?

TRAVELING LIGHT

*In order to be anointed…
let the shepherd do his work.*

# My Cup Runs Over

Is an overflowing cup full? Absolutely. The wine reaches the rim and then tumbles over the edge. The goblet is not large enough to contain the quantity. According to David, our hearts are not large enough to contain the blessings that God wants to give. He pours and pours until they literally flow over the edge and down on the table.

The overflowing cup was a powerful symbol in the days of David. Hosts in the ancient East used it to send a message to the guest. As long as the cup was kept full, the guest knew he was welcome. But when the cup sat empty, the host was hinting that the hour was late. On those occasions, however, when the host really enjoyed the company of the person, he filled the cup to overflowing. He didn't stop when the wine reached the rim; he kept pouring until the liquid ran over the edge of the cup and down the table.[5]

TRAVELING LIGHT

Have you ever wondered why God gives so much? We could exist on far less. He could have left the world flat and gray; we wouldn't have known the difference. But he didn't.

> *He splashed orange in the sunrise*
> *    and cast the sky in blue.*
> *And if you love to see geese as they gather,*
> *    chances are you'll see that too.*
> *Did he have to make the squirrel's tail furry?*
> *Was he obliged to make the birds sing?*
> *And the funny way that chickens scurry*
> *    or the majesty of thunder when it rings?*
> *Why give a flower fragrance? Why give food*
> *    its taste?*
> *Could it be*
> *    he loves to see*
> *    that look upon your face?*

*If we give gifts to show our love, how much more would he?*

If we give gifts to show our love, how much more would he? If we—speckled with foibles and greed—love to give gifts, how much more does God, pure and perfect God, enjoy giving gifts to us?

HE CHOSE THE NAILS

So the next time a sunrise steals your breath or a meadow of flowers leaves you speechless, remain that way. Say nothing and listen as heaven whispers, "Do you like it? I did it just for you."

I'm about to tell you something you may find hard to believe.... Here it is: If you were the only person on earth, the earth would look exactly the same. The Himalayas would still have their drama and the Caribbean would still have its charm. The sun would still nestle behind the Rockies in the evenings and spray light on the desert mornings. If you were the sole pilgrim on this globe, God would not diminish its beauty one degree.

Because he did it all for you...and he's waiting for you to discover his gift.... He's waiting for your eyes to pop and your heart to stop. He's waiting for the moment between the dropping of the jaw and the leap of the heart. For in the silence he leans forward and whispers: I did it just for you.

Find such love hard to believe? That's okay.... Just because we can't imagine God giving us sunsets, don't think God doesn't do it. God's thoughts are higher than ours. God's ways are greater than ours. And sometimes, out of his great wisdom, our Father in heaven gives us a piece of heaven just to show he cares.

THE GREAT HOUSE OF GOD

# Surely Goodness and Mercy Shall Follow Me All the Days of My Life

Goodness to supply every want.
Mercy to forgive every sin.
Goodness to provide.
Mercy to pardon.

—F. B. Meyer

"S̲u̲r̲e̲l̲y̲ g̲o̲o̲d̲n̲e̲s̲s̲ and mercy shall follow me all the days of my life" (Psalm 23:6).

This must be one of the sweetest phrases ever penned. Can we read it from a few other translations?

> "Goodness and love unfailing, these will follow me all the days of my life, and I shall dwell in the house of the Lord my whole life" (NEB).

> "I know that your goodness and love will be with me all my life; and your house will be my home as long as I live" (TEV).

> "Your beauty and love chase after me every day of my life. I'm back home in the house of God for the rest of my life" (MSG).

To read the verse is to open a box of jewels. Each word sparkles and begs to be examined in the face of our doubts: *goodness, mercy, all the days, dwell in the house of the LORD forever.* They sweep in on insecurities like a SWAT team on a terrorist.

Look at the first word: *surely.* David didn't say, "*Maybe* goodness and mercy shall follow me." Or "*Possibly* goodness and mercy shall follow me." Or "I have a hunch that goodness and mercy shall follow me." David could have used one of those phrases. But he didn't. He believed in a sure God, who makes sure promises and provides a sure foundation.

Our moods may shift, but God doesn't. Our minds may change, but God doesn't. Our devotion may falter, but God's never does. Even if we are faithless, he is faithful, for he cannot betray himself (2 Timothy 2:13). He is a sure God. And because he is a sure God, we can state confidently, "Surely goodness and mercy shall follow me all the days of my life."

And what follows the word *surely?* "Goodness and mercy." If the Lord is the shepherd who leads the flock, goodness and mercy are the two sheepdogs that guard the rear of the flock. Goodness *and* mercy. Not goodness alone, for we are sinners in need of mercy. Not mercy alone, for we are fragile, in need of goodness. We need them both.

Goodness and mercy—the celestial escort of God's flock. If that duo doesn't reinforce your faith, try this phrase: "all the days of my life."

What a huge statement. Look at the size of it! Goodness and mercy follow the child of God each and every day! Think of the days that lie ahead. What do you see? Days at home with only toddlers? God will be at your side. Days in a dead-end job? He will walk you through. Days of loneliness? He will take your hand. Surely goodness and mercy shall follow me—not some, not most, not nearly all—but *all* the days of my life.

And what will he do during those days? (Here is my favorite word.) He will "follow" you.

What a surprising way to describe a God who remains in one place. A God who sits enthroned in the heavens and rules and ordains. David, however, envisions a mobile and active God. Dare we do the same? Dare we envision a God who follows us?

*Release your doubts.*
*Set them down.*
*You can trust God.*

Who pursues us? Who chases us? Who tracks us down and wins us over? Who follows us with "goodness and mercy" all the days of our lives?...

God is the God who follows. I wonder…have you sensed him following you? We often miss him. We don't know our Helper when he is near. But he comes.

Through the kindness of a stranger. The majesty of a sunset. The mystery of romance. Through the question of a child or the commitment of a spouse. Through a word well spoken or a touch well timed, have you sensed his presence? If so, then release your doubts. Set them down. Be encumbered by them no longer. You are no candidate for insecurity. You are no longer a client of timidity. You can trust God. He has given his love to you; why don't you give your doubts to him?...

God gives us himself. Even when we choose our hovel over his house and our trash over his grace, still he follows. Never forcing us. Never leaving us. Patiently persistent. Faithfully present. Using all of his power to convince us that he is who he is and that he can be trusted to lead us home.

His goodness and mercy follow us all the days of our lives.

TRAVELING LIGHT

# I Will Dwell in the House of the Lord Forever

This isn't just any house.
It is our Father's house.

WHERE WILL YOU live forever? In the house of the Lord. If his house is your "forever house," what does that make this earthly house? You got it! Short-term housing. This is not our home. "Our homeland is in heaven" (Philippians 3:20).

This explains the homesickness we feel.

Have you ever longed to be home? May I share a time when I did? I was spending the summer of my nineteenth year working in northern Georgia. The folks in that region are very nice, but no one is too nice to a door-to-door salesman. There were times that summer when I was so lonely for home I felt my bones would melt.

One of those occasions came on the side of a country road. The hour was late, I was lost. I'd stopped to pull out a flashlight and a map. To my right was a farmhouse. In the farmhouse was a family. I knew it was a family because I could see them. Right through the big plate-glass window, I could see the mother and father and boy and girl. Norman Rockwell would have placed them on a canvas. The mom was spooning out food, and the dad was telling a story, and the kids were laughing, and it was all I could do to keep from ringing the doorbell and asking for a place at the table. I felt so far from home.

What I felt that night, some of you have felt ever since...

Your husband died.

Your child was buried.

You learned about the lump in your breast or the spot on your lung.

Some of you have felt far from home ever since your home fell apart.

The twists and turns of life have a way of reminding us—we aren't home here. This is not our homeland. We aren't fluent in the languages of disease and death. The culture confuses the heart, the noise disrupts our sleep, and we feel far from home.

And, you know what? That's OK.

You have an eternal address fixed in your mind. God has "set eternity in the hearts of men" (Ecclesiastes 3:11 NIV). Down deep you know you are not home yet.

So be careful not to act like you are.

TRAVELING LIGHT

*God never said that the journey would be easy, but he did say that the arrival would be worthwhile.*

Though our eyes are fixed on heaven, for some of us the journey has been long. Very long and stormy. In no way do I wish to minimize the difficulties that you have had to face along the way. Some of you have shouldered burdens that few of us could ever carry. You have bid farewell to lifelong partners. You have been robbed of lifelong dreams. You have been given bodies that can't sustain your spirit. You have spouses who can't tolerate your faith. You have bills that outnumber the paychecks and challenges that outweigh the strength.

And you are tired.

It's hard for you to see the city in the midst of the storms. The desire to pull over to the side of the road and get out entices you. You want to go on, but some days the road seems so long.

Remember this: God never said that the journey would be easy, but he did say that the arrival would be worthwhile. He may not do what you want, but he will do what is right…and best. He's the Father of forward motion. Trust him. He will get you home. And the trials of the trip will be lost in the joys of the feast.

In the Eye of the Storm

# Closing Thoughts

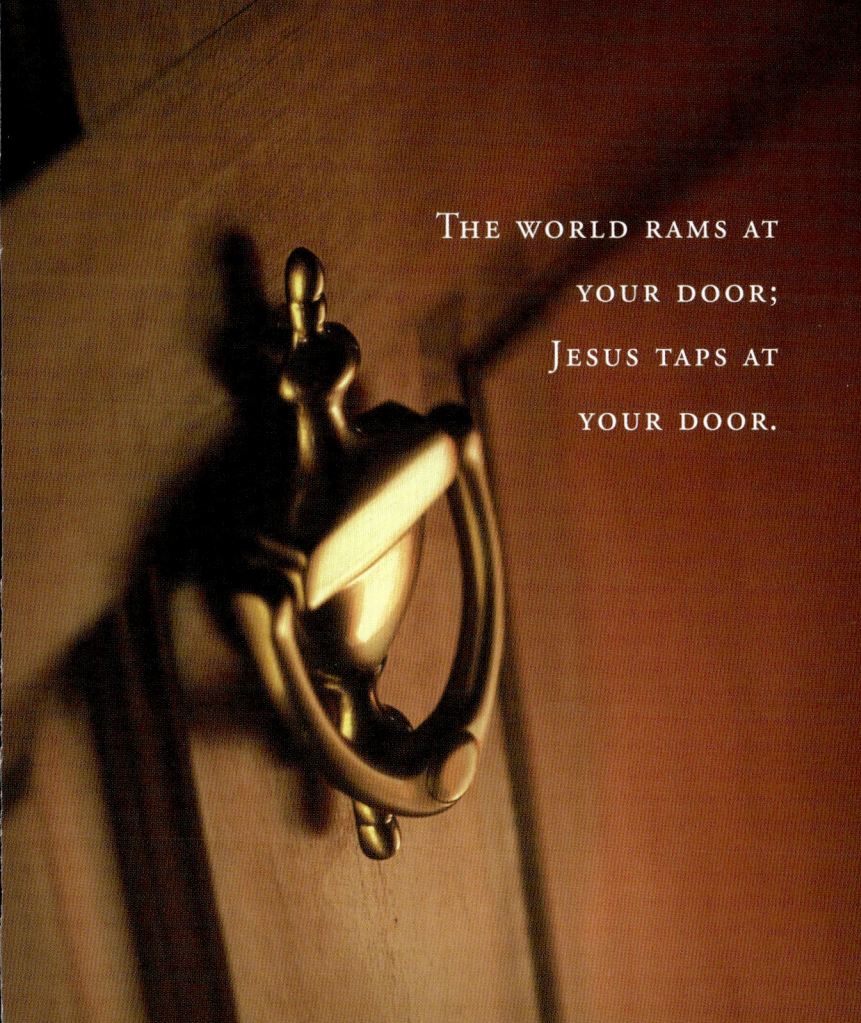

THE MARK OF A SHEEP is its ability to hear the shepherd's voice.

"The sheep listen to his voice. He calls his own sheep by name and leads them out" (John 10:3 NIV).

The mark of a disciple is his or her ability to hear the Master's voice.

"Here I am! I stand at the door and knock. If anyone hears my voice and opens the door, I will come in and eat with him, and he with me" (Revelation 3:20 NLT).

The world rams at your door; Jesus taps at your door. The voices scream for your allegiance; Jesus softly and tenderly requests it. The world promises flashy pleasure; Jesus promises a quiet dinner…with God. "I will come in and eat."

Which voice do you hear?

*There is never a time during which Jesus is not speaking nor a place in which Jesus is not present.*

Let me state something important. There is never a time during which Jesus is not speaking. Never. There is never a place in which Jesus is not present. Never. There is never a room so dark…a lounge so sensual…an office so sophisticated…that the ever-present, ever-pursuing, relentlessly tender Friend is not there, tapping gently on the doors of our hearts—waiting to be invited in.

Few hear his voice. Fewer still open the door.

But never interpret our numbness as his absence. For amidst the fleeting promises of pleasure is the timeless promise of his presence.

"Surely, I am with you always, to the very end of the age" (Matthew 28:20 NIV).

"Never will I leave you; never will I forsake you" (Hebrews 13:5 NIV).

There is no chorus so loud that the voice of God cannot be heard…if we will but listen….

A day is coming when everyone will hear his voice. A day is coming when all the other voices will be silenced; his voice—and his voice only—will be heard.

Some will hear his voice for the very first time. It's not that he never spoke; it's just that they never listened. For these, God's voice will be the voice of a stranger. They will hear it once—and never hear it again. They will spend eternity fending off the voices they followed on earth.

But others will be called from their graves by a familiar voice. For they are sheep who know their Shepherd. They are servants who opened the door when Jesus knocked.

Now the door will be open again. Only this time, it won't be Jesus who walks into our house; it will be we, who walk into his.

IN THE EYE OF THE STORM

# 30-DAY DEVOTIONAL

# God's Comfort

*Even if I walk through a very dark valley,*
*I will not be afraid,*
*because you are with me.*
*Your rod and your shepherd's staff comfort me.*

Psalm 23:4

There are historical moments in which a real God met real pain so we could answer the question, "Where is God when it hurts?"

How does God react to you when you are hurting? Do you long for God to speak to your lonely heart?

The God who spoke still speaks… The God who came still comes. He comes into our world. He comes into your world. He comes to do what you can't.

*Our hearts are not large enough to contain the blessings that God wants to give.*

Hope Pure & Simple

## Never Give Up on God

*God always does what he says
and is gracious in everything he does.*

PSALM 145:13 MSG

God never gives up. When Moses said,
"Here I am, send Aaron," God didn't give up....
When Peter worshipped him at the supper
and cursed him at the fire, he didn't give up....

So the next time doubt walks into your life,
remember the cross, where in holy blood is written
the promise: "God would give up his only Son
before he'd give up on you."

*God's faithfulness has never depended on
the faithfulness of his children.
He is faithful even when we aren't.*

Hope Pure & Simple

# Footprints on Your Heart—
# God's Simple Reminders

*LORD, teach me what you want me to do,*
*and I will live by your truth.*

PSALM 86:11

When kindness comes grudgingly, we'll remember God's kindness to us and ask him to make us more kind. When patience is scarce, thank him for his and ask him to make us more patient. When it's hard to forgive, we won't list all the times we've given grief. Rather, we'll list all the times we've been given grace and pray to become more forgiving.

*Catalog God's goodness.*
*Meditate on them.*
*He has fed you, led you, and earned your trust.*
*Remember what God has done for you.*

Hope Pure & Simple

# Be Still—He Is with You

> *I will meditate on the glorious splendor of Your majesty and on Your wondrous works.*
> Psalm 145:5 NKJV

Has it been a while since you stared at the heavens in speechless amazement? Has it been awhile since you realized God's divinity?…
If it has, then you need to know something.
He is still there and always will be. He hasn't left.
Under all those papers and books and reports and years. In the midst of all those voices and faces and memories and pictures….

He is still there.

*God knows your beginning and your end because he has neither.*

Hope Pure & Simple

# A Shepherd at All Times

> *You are all around me—in front and in back—and have put your hand on me.*
> PSALM 139:5

We wonder with so many miraculous testimonies around us, how we could escape God. But somehow we do. We live in an art gallery of creativity yet are content to gaze only at the carpenter.

The next time you see a baby laugh or see an ocean wave, take note. Pause and listen as his majesty ever so gently whispers, "I'm here."

*You may feel alone in the wilderness, but you are not; God is with you.*

Hope Pure & Simple

# You Have Value…Just as You Are

*With your very own hands you formed me;*
*now breathe your wisdom over me.*

PSALM 119:73 MSG

Listen closely, Jesus' love does
not depend upon what we do for him.
Not at all. In the eye of the King,
you have value simply because you are.
You don't have to look nice or perform well.
Your value is inborn.

You are valuable…not because of what you do
or what you have done, but simply because you are.
Remember that.

*God takes you however he finds you.*
*No need to clean up or climb up. Just look up.*

Hope Pure & Simple

# You Matter

*God, examine me and know my heart;…*
*Lead me on the road to everlasting life.*
PSALM 139:23–24

You don't have to be like the world to have an impact on the world. You don't have to be like the crowd to change the crowd. You don't have to lower yourself down to their level to lift them up to your level.

Holiness doesn't seek to be odd. Holiness seeks to be like God.

*With God, every day matters, every person counts. And that includes you.*

Hope Pure & Simple

# The Ultimate Choice

*I have chosen the way of truth;*
*I have set my heart on your laws.*

Psalm 119:30 niv

Think about it. There are many things in life
that we can't choose. We can't, for example,
choose the weather. We can't control the economy.
We can't choose whether or not we are born
with a big nose, blue eyes, or a lot of hair….

But we can choose where we spend eternity.
The big choice, God leaves to us.

*God invites us to love Him. He urges us to love Him.*
*But in the end, the choice is yours and mine.*

Hope Pure & Simple

## Looking for Real Change

*Create in me a new, clean heart, O God.*
Psalm 51:10 TLB

Ever blame life's problems on the issues and circumstances of the day? What about trying to resolve them? No matter if its business or more personally related, consider the prayer of David, "Create in me a new heart, O God."…

Real change is an inside job. You might alter things in a day or two with money and systems, but the heart of the matter is and will always be, a matter of the heart.

*A problem is no more a challenge to God than a twig is to an elephant.*

Hope Pure & Simple

# Fill Your Heart with God's Grace

*Do good to me, your servant, so I can live, so I can obey your word.*
Psalm 119:17

God loves to decorate. God has to decorate. Let him live long enough in a heart, and that heart will begin to change. Portraits of hurt will be replaced with landscapes of grace.

Walls of anger will be demolished and shaky foundations restored. God can no more leave a life unchanged than a mother can leave her child's tear untouched.

*What is grace? It's what someone gives us out of the goodness of his heart, not out of the perfection of ours.*

Hope Pure & Simple

# God's Faithfulness

*I will always be about the Lord's love;*
*I will tell of his loyalty from now on.*
*I will say, "Your love continues forever;*
*your loyalty goes on and on like the sky.*
Psalms 89:1–2

We are God's idea. We are his. His face. His eyes. His hands. His touch. We are him. Look deeply into the face of every human being on earth, and you will see his likeness. Though some appear to be distant relatives, they are not. God has no cousins, only children.

We are incredibly, the body of Christ. And though we may not act like our Father, there is no greater truth than this: We are his. Unalterably, he loves us. Undyingly. Nothing can separate us from the love of Christ.

*Rest today in the knowledge that you are precious to the One who matters most. Nothing can alter that fact. Nothing.*

# Who Are You Going to Trust?

*You answer us in amazing ways, God our Savior.*

Psalm 65:5

God never turns his back on those who ask
honest questions. He never did in the Old Testament;
he never did in the New Testament.
So if you are asking honest questions of God,
he will not turn away from you…

In learning to depend on God, we must accept
that we may not know all the answers,
but we know who knows the answers.

*We must trust God.
We must trust not only that he does what is best
but that he knows what is ahead.*

Hope Pure & Simple

# Letting Sin Go

*He forgives your sins—every one.*

Psalm 103:3 msg

It's against God's nature to remember forgiven sins....

He who is perfect love cannot hold grudges.
If he does, then he isn't perfect love.
And if he isn't perfect love,
you might as well put this book down and go fishing,
because both of us are chasing fairytales.

But I believe in his loving forgetfulness.
And I believe he has a graciously terrible memory.

*Place your mistake before the judgment seat of God.*
*Let Him condemn it, let Him pardon it, and put it away.*

Hope Pure & Simple

## Our Protection Plan

> *Pile your troubles on God's shoulders—*
> *he'll carry your load.*
> PSALM 55:22 MSG

I wonder how many burdens Jesus is carrying for us that we know nothing about? We're aware of some. He carries our sin. He carries our shame. He carries our eternal debt. But are there others?

Has he lifted fears before we felt them?... Those times when we have been surprised by our own sense of peace? Could it be that Jesus has lifted our anxiety onto his shoulders and placed a yoke of kindness on ours?

*It's time to let God's love cover all things in our life. All secrets. All hurts.*

Hope Pure & Simple

# Seeing the Glass Half Full

*The LORD God is like a sun and shield;*
*the LORD gives us kindness and honor.*

PSALM 84:11

Rejections are like speed bumps on the road.
They come with the journey....
You can't keep people from rejecting you.
But you can keep rejections from enraging you.
How? By letting God's acceptance compensate
for their rejection.

When others reject you, let God accept you.
He is not frowning. He is not mad. He sings over you.
Take a long drink from his limitless love.

*Does your self-esteem ever sag?*
*When it does, remember what you are worth.*

Hope Pure & Simple

# Sealed in His Love

*Thank you for your love,
thank you for your faithfulness.*
Psalm 138:2 msg

We give more applause to a brawny ball-carrier than we do the God who made us. We sing more songs to the moon than we do to the Christ who saves us....

Though we may not act like our Father, there is no greater truth than this: We are his. Unalterably. He loves us. Undyingly.

*The love of people often increases with performance and decreases with mistakes. Not so with God's love.*

Hope Pure & Simple

# Relying on God's Promise

*Surely goodness and mercy shall follow me all the days of my life, and I will dwell in the house of the Lord forever.*

Psalm 23:6 nkjv

What a huge statement. Look at the size of it! Goodness and mercy follow the child of God each and every day! Think of the days that lie ahead. What do you see? Days at home with only toddlers? God will be at your side. Days in a dead-end job? He will walk you through. Days of loneliness? He will take your hand.

Surely goodness and mercy shall follow me—not some, not most, not nearly all—but all the days of my life.

*If God can make a billion galaxies, can't He make good out of our bad and sense out of our faltering lives? Of course He can. He is God.*

Hope Pure & Simple

# No Greater Love

*When I was desperate, I called out,
and God got me out of a tight spot.*

Psalm 34:6 msg

Run to Jesus. Jesus wants you to go to him.
He wants to become the most important
person in your life,
the greatest love you'll ever know.

He wants you to love him so much that there's
no room in your heart and in your life for sin.
Invite him to take up residence in your heart.

*How wide is God's love?
Wide enough for the whole world.*

Hope Pure & Simple

# Take Time to Notice…
# God Is at Work

*The testimony of the LORD is sure,*
*making wise the simple.*

PSALM 19:7 NKJV

"God's testimony," wrote David,
"makes wise the simple."

God's testimony.
When was the last time you witnessed it?
A stroll through knee-high grass in a green meadow.
An hour listening to seagulls or…
witnessing the rays of sunlight brighten the snow
on a crisp winter dawn.

Miracles…happen all around us;
we only have to pay attention.

*God always rejoices when we dare to dream.*

Hope Pure & Simple

# Home Team Advantage

*God is the strength of my heart.*
Psalm 73:26 nkjv

God is for you. Turn to the sidelines; that's God cheering you on. Look past the finish line; that's God applauding your steps. Listen for him in the bleachers, shouting your name. Too tired to continue?

He'll carry you. Too discouraged to fight? He's picking you up. God is for you.

*Our devotion may falter, but God's never does.*

Hope Pure & Simple

# Give God Your Worries

*When I kept things to myself,
I felt weak deep inside me.*
Psalm 32:3

Ask yourself:

*Are there any unsurrendered worries in my heart?*

"Give all your worries to him, because he cares about you" (I Peter 5:7).

The German word for *worry* means "to strangle." The Greek word means "to divide the mind." Both are accurate. Worry is a noose on the neck and a distraction of the mind, neither of which is befitting for joy.

*God is leading you. Leave tomorrow's problems until tomorrow.*

Hope Pure & Simple

# God's Plans

*Enjoy serving the LORD,*
*and he will give you what you want.*

PSALM 37:4

When we submit to God's plans, we can trust
our desires. Our assignment is found at the intersection
of God's plan and our pleasures.

Some long to feed the poor.
Others enjoy leading the church…
Each of us have been made to serve God in a unique way…

The longings of your heart, then, are not incidental;
they are critical messages.
The desires of your heart are not to be ignored;
they are to be consulted.

*We must trust God.*
*We must trust not only that he does what is best,*
*but that he knows what is ahead.*

Hope Pure & Simple

## Your Whispering Thoughts

*God, examine me and know my heart; test me and know my anxious thoughts.*
Psalm 139:23

Imagine considering every moment as a potential time of communion with God. By the time your life is over, you will have spent six months at stoplights, eight months opening junk mail, a year and a half looking for lost articles, and approximately five years standing in various lines.

Why don't you give these moments to God instead? By giving God your whispering thoughts, the common become uncommon. Just pray where you are. Give God more of your daily thoughts.

*Within reach of your prayers is the maker of the oceans—God!*

Hope Pure & Simple

# Intimacy with the Almighty

*As a deer thirsts for streams of water,*
*so I thirst for you, God.*

Psalm 42:1

Jesus didn't act unless he saw his Father act.
He didn't judge until he heard his Father judge.
No act or deed occurred without his Father's guidance….

Because Jesus could hear what others couldn't,
he acted differently than they did.
Do you suppose the Father desires the same for us?
Absolutely! God desires the same
abiding intimacy with you that he had with his Son.

*Christ is in you!*
*Your heart is his home, and he is your master.*

Hope Pure & Simple

# God's Passion and Plan

*Your word is like a lamp for my feet
and a light for my path.*

PSALM 119:105

The purpose of the Bible is simply
to proclaim God's plan to save his children.
It asserts that man is lost and needs to be saved.
And it communicates the message that
Jesus is God in the flesh sent to save his children.

What a truth! Understanding the purpose of the Bible
is like seeing the compass in the right direction.
Calibrate it correctly, and you'll journey safely.
But fail to see it, and who knows where you'll end up.

*God leads us. He will do the right thing at the right time.*

Hope Pure & Simple

# Character Creates Courage

*All you who put your hope in the LORD be strong and brave.*
PSALM 31:24

How many people do you know who have built a formidable exterior only to tremble inside with fear? We face our fears with force, or we stockpile wealth. We seek security in things. We cultivate fame and seek status.

But do these approaches work?

Courage is an outgrowth of who we are. Exterior supports may temporarily sustain, but only inward character creates courage.

*Whatever you are facing, God knows how you feel.*

# A Cut Above

*Be still, and know that I am God.*
PSALM 46:10 NIV

The word *holy* means "to separate." The ancestry of the term can be tracked back to the ancient meaning, "to cut." To be holy, then, is to be a cut above the norm, superior, extraordinary…

The Holy One dwells on a different level than the rest of us. What frightens us does not frighten him. What troubles us does not trouble him.

When you set your sights on our God, you focus on One "a cut above" any storm life may bring…. You find peace.

*You cannot be anything you want to be. But you can be everything God wants you to be.*

Hope Pure & Simple

# See What God Has Done!

*The heavens declare the Glory of God.*

PSALM 19:1

How vital that we pray armed with the knowledge
that God is in heaven. Pray with any lesser conviction
and your prayers are timid, shallow, and hollow.

But spend some time walking in the workshop
of the heavens, seeing what God has done,
and watch how your prayers are energized.

By showing us the heavens,
Jesus is showing us his Father's workshop....
He taps us on the shoulder and says,
"Your Father can handle that for you."

*Your prayers are honored as precious jewels.
Your words do not stop until they reach the very throne of God.*

Hope Pure & Simple

# A Home for Your Heart

*LORD, I love the Temple where you live, where your glory is.*

PSALM 26:8

When it comes to resting your soul, there is no place like the Great House of God. If you could ask God for one thing, what would you request?

David tells us what he would ask. He longs to *live* in the house of God. The word *live* is emphasized because it deserves to be emphasized. David doesn't want to chat. He doesn't desire a cup of coffee on the back porch. He doesn't ask for a meal or to spend an evening in God's house, rather he longs to retire there.

David isn't seeking a temporary assignment, but rather a lifelong residence.

*If you want to touch God's heart,
use the name he loves to hear. Call him* Father.

# God's Help Is Near

> *The LORD is close to everyone who prays to him,
> to all who truly pray to him.*
> PSALM 145:18

Healing begins when we do something…when we take that first step. God's help is near and always available, but it is only given to those who seek it. Nothing results from apathy…

God honors radical, risk-taking faith. But it takes someone doing something in order to see results.

What is God revealing to you? What is something you need to act on in order to have the Lord stop and respond? It's never too late to seek him— no matter what the need or request is.

*God's help is near and always available, but it is only given to those who seek it.*

## ENDNOTES

1. Donald W. McCullough, *The Trivialization of God: The Dangerous Illusion of a Manageable Deity* (Colorado Springs: NavPress, 1995), 66.

2. From "Worrier and Warrior," a sermon by Ted Schroder, Christ Episcopal Church, San Antonio, Texas, on 10 April 1994.

3. Charles W. Slemming, *He Leadeth Me: The Shepherd's Life in Palestine,* (Fort Washington, PA.: Christian Literature Crusade, 1964), quoted in Charles R. Swindoll, *Living Beyond the Daily Grind, Book 1: Reflections on the Songs and Saying in Scripture* (Dallas: Word Publishing, 1988), 77–78.

4. Phillip Keller, *A Shepherd's Look at Psalm 23* (Grand Rapids, Mich.: Zondervan Publishing, 1970; reprint, in Phillip Keller: *The Inspirational Writings,* New York: Inspirational Press, 1993).

## ACKNOWLEDGMENTS

Grateful acknowledgment is made to the following publishers for permission to reprint this copyrighted material. All copyrights are held by the author, Max Lucado.

*The Applause of Heaven* (Nashville: Word, 1990).
*In the Eye of the Storm* (Nashville: Word, 1991).
*He Still Moves Stones* (Nashville: Word, 1993).
*When God Whispers Your Name* (Nashville: Word, 1994).
*A Gentle Thunder* (Nashville: Word, 1995).
*In the Grip of Grace* (Nashville: Word, 1996).
*The Great House of God* (Nashville: Word, 1997).
*He Chose the Nails* (Nashville: Word, 2000).
*Traveling Light* (Nashville: Word, 2000).
*"He Reminded Us of You"* (a prayer for a friend).
*Grace for the Moment Volume 1* (Nashville: Thomas Nelson, 2000).
*Everyday Blessings* (Nashville: Thomas Nelson, 2006).
*Hope, Pure and Simple* (Nashville: Thomas Nelson, 2007).